LETTERS TO HER;
LETTERS TO NO ONE

by

Ian Bagley

Letters to Her; Letters to No One

© 2016 Ian Bagley. All rights reserved.

First Edition

ISBN: 978-1523322619

This book is a recollection of one man's viewpoint. As such, names and places have been changed to protect all of those involved.

Cover illustration by Kiriska © 2016. All rights reserved.

www.kiriska.com

Special thanks to Derek and Elizabeth for your tireless work with me on making things tighter and more cohesive.

Thanks to Darryl for saving my life.

Thanks to Mom and Sherry for always being so kind and loving.

Thanks to Kathie for your wisdom and reminding me that my life matters and to John for putting up with a random third son.

Thanks to Dad and Paul for showing me how to be a man – even if I screw up.

Thanks to Rhiannon, Ryan, Spencer, Nathon, all nine of my grandparents, and to everyone that shares blood with me.

Thanks to Kurt, Jason, David and Jeff for being so understanding and tolerating what I've been going through, and your comradery.

Thanks to Dana for reminding me to choose joy.

Chelsea for encouraging me and being straightforward when you had to be.

Thanks to Hayley, Jess, Jules, Bri, Sylvia, Kali, Max, Dana, Jax, Hanna, Paul, Colin, David, Skye, Rich, Hannah, Pac, Mandy, Jay and Natalie

To Debbie

From Ian

Dedicated to the girl with the mahogany eyes, who took my breath away and made me know what living really feels like. To the girl I harmed: these words are for you.

-LI

LETTERS TO HER; LETTERS TO NO ONE

These are my letters
To her
With mahogany eyes
Deserving all I could give
More
Whose worth exceeded my capacity
To precisely perceive the dichotomy
Doze in my arms, let go
Grasping every wonderful whim
Smiling somewhere, my favorite smile
My most beloved eyes, hair
Somewhere
Far off; unattainable by my own selfish need
While I sit here, deftly defining greed
Whose perfect opalescent orbs observe Brighter horizons
With someone else to share, anyone else
But no longer me
No longer the confidant
The trusted ear; the comforter
Instead a dissipating, destructive dispenser of old advice
Of adages, for savages like myself
Disposed of and left blistering in the sun
Until I am unable to carry on, soon carrion
Circle 'round my head, my death bed,
Nothing but these words left
These letters to her
But she is not who she was anymore
That love, dead
She is gone
Only these letters remain
These letters to no one

Letters to Her; Letters to No One
MAHOGANY EYES

Make the clouds relinquish the skies
Just a glance, the tension relaxes - sighs
Those perfect brown eyes wrest time still
An indescribable thrill
That jolt, that peering,
It hastens the heart
Just from seeing her lips part
But I could spend minutes
Hours
Even days
Beholden to that enveloping gaze

Letters to Her; Letters to No One
December 13th

Dear No One,

    Happy birthday. It's a big day for you, and I regret that I cannot be there to share in your celebration

    I remember our plans for the 16th, when we would go to the science center. I hope your brother takes you instead.

    I hope you're showered with every bit of love and adoration you deserve.

Yours truly,
Ian

Letters to Her; Letters to No One
OFFERING

A pot in a museum
The class of children
Walks past
Just another pot
Some old, ancient, worn piece
Cracked down one half
The small etchings barely visible
A pot
That had little to offer then
And nothing now

Letters to Her; Letters to No One
THE QUIET CONGREGATION

Even the most stentorian sentence can stagnate in the presence of a symphony

The power of the many meek overpowering the mighty one

But more powerful than the greatest uproar
The silent jury that cannot be swayed

Letters to Her; Letters to No One
CANDLE

I stand, wavering
One crimson candle in the clouds,
An errant, ancient lamp
She sees me, "A star? No, not so far"

Will she deliver the bleak truth I seek?
I flicker, vulnerable to her inebriating influence
My failing, fiery eye doesn't hide
She approaches me in the sky
I light that flawless, fearless face

Pucker your lips and blow, I beg
or with a pinch, snuff me out
I seek the silent solitude, a sanctuary
But with you nearby, the gales cease
And finally
I stand, firm

Letters to Her; Letters to No One
December 25th

Dear No One,

It's Christmas today. I pray your family is well and enjoys the exchange. Not just of gifts but love.

You are on my mind much this season. I had plans; so many ideas for gifts for you.

We would have been out in the open by now. My mind likes to abuse me with that thought.

I had gotten you a harmonica with your name engraved on it. Well, at least your initials. I got it just before you left me.

The night before I went to the hospital, I had stared at it and smiled. "God wouldn't let me invest this much of myself without saving me," I foolishly thought. I even started work on the wood carving I had mentioned before.

When I got back home, I turned the carving to ash and donated the instrument.

When will this hell end? Who knows? But even the good memories are only bittersweet.

Merry Christmas,
Ian

Letters to Her; Letters to No One
COLUMNS PT. I

I went back
To the fictional place we'd made
Closed my eyes and saw the sun
My face caressed by its warmth
I miss the arcane chill
The lost lover's embrace
Time apart but united by heart
In this field of clovers
Clouds part
Winds bellow, tossing leaves
Rays of light pierce
Ominous clouds
I am alone here
Next to the columns
Where I have been waiting
Two fallen pillars
Make an X in front of me
Where you should be
As vines grow and creep
Standing watchful
Never sleeping
I pray my vigilance will be
Rewarded

Letters to Her; Letters to No One
ICE PICK

You think you're so slick with that ice pick
Aroused by the way my skull splits
All the precious pits in your stomach
When you chain me to that welded wall
You pray someday I'll go away
But you're the cause of my fall
Fickle with that sickle, you strike again
Right on the chin, like a subterranean
Atrocity, mocking me, flogging me
Plausible deniability
Now just invoiced into debt
In the red, O negative
All over your brittle little boots
Your skeletal hands wrapped briskly
Over my husk of a heart
Bandages tattered from all the times I fell apart
Rescind, react, restart
Strike again like a fiercely fidelic smith
Hammer it harmoniously
Impact every shard
Like a constellation of consolations
Fan it out like a deck of cards
Pick one, any one, the trick is the same
Sequestered in your youth, I was
Ignorant
How dare I react to the things I discovered
No matter how despicable or dastardly
Treat me like a criminal
As if it wasn't of your own volition
That you didn't love me
I'd never be validated
Instead imprisoned in memories
Buried between the sheets

Letters to Her; Letters to No One

Then sink that blade deep, so it seeps
And covers up the lover's marks
You weren't panting my name
The only one that made a mistake
Was me

Letters to Her; Letters to No One
December 26th

Dear No One,

  It's raining a lot today. I'm at the pub and I can't help but remember the night of the fireflies.
  Do you remember that night? It was possibly the best night in my twenty-seven years on this Earth.
  The sights, the sounds, the smell of you and the feeling of your diminutive weight in my arms. That was when I knew I needed nothing else. Wanted nothing else.
  To see those eyes widen in awe, those lips part in the greatest smile I have ever witnessed. That was all I wanted in this world.
  I want to forget it. I don't want to forget it.
  I need to escape this nightmare. The day-in, day-out spent in an air-conditioned hell, unable to go more than an hour without you popping up.
  This is a true prison. I cannot escape, and the fact is that the memories that meant something so long ago will evaporate and mean nothing later on. This is something I must come to terms with. Maybe you can show me how.

Regards,
Ian

Letters to Her; Letters to No One
ROAD CLOSED

Rushing water closed the road
A sign boldly states
I utter my frustrations
But you don't miss a beat
Park the car
Get on your feet
I follow
We're under the stars

I'm still inebriated
You come to my side
I smother you with affection
We separate
You stare, eyes widen
I shift my gaze to up above
To see a cloud of fireflies

The words we utter don't do it justice
To have so many tiny miracles among us
Entirely enamored, you're entranced
As they danced, you smile my favorite smile

While you're feeling blessed by the view
I feel blessed by holding you

Letters to Her; Letters to No One
COORDINATES

Fears manifest and surround me
Anxiety gets my heart pounding
Down to the depths
It's peculiar
Your eyes were so crepuscular
Now sinister
Precisely when they close that clean casket
Lower it into the ground
You'll be astounded
Relieved, but so desperate
To finish the job
You roll up your sleeves
Bury me
So I disappear, fearing what I might say
You just pray that someday you'll forget
This place
And the location of
My grave

Letters to Her; Letters to No One
TREE

An old oak tree stands and watches over his neighborhood
On the corner of First and Sage Avenue
He carves their names into its trunk
Its body bleeds, slowly sap seeps
But it doesn't cry
Their first kiss is under its branches
On a brisk autumn day
The tree watches them go off without word
It's worried but it fades, four years later
They return
The Sun has set and risen how many times since they first kissed?
And now they're making vows
The old tree still stands watching
They make promises in its presence
Years pass and their children play
Picnics on a Saturday afternoon
The mother comforts her newest born
A cloud or two threatens to ruin their day
But not a drop bothers them
As its arms are splayed out over them
It protects them as much as he can
The husband and wife argue a bit, a tiff
The oak can do nothing but hope
It watches the wife come home
Later and later
Less lively, less loving
But more lovely
The husband visits the old tree, weeping its tears
Traces his fingers on the carving of their names
The sun sets, and when it rises
The man is left dangling
On the corner of First and Sage Avenue

Letters to Her; Letters to No One
December 28th

Dear No One,

You once said, "There is nothing but this." While I know you hate me now for the terrible things I did, is there any chance that we can reconcile down the road?

I'm drinking, so that's why I want to know. I need to know.

But I know there isn't hope. All I can have is Faith.

"Not my will, but thine." I have had to say this to myself every day. It is the only thing that brings me any semblance of comfort.

That I might have some purpose. That maybe I was built this way for a reason. I am a struggler, after all. I contend. I fought and struggled for you. I would fight endlessly through the greatest pains you can summon in your head. All for No One. For the best person I have ever known.

This must be the booze talking. Here's to you, No One!

Cheers!
Ian

Letters to Her; Letters to No One
A BEACON, A BLAZE

She is powerful and bright
Not just a spark in the dark
But a pillar of light
In this radiance, I saw all I desired
Not something I conceived, just believed
Faith stoked the fire
Hope fed the flames
I tried to ignore what my life was for
Eyes upon the heavens, I heard them whisper our names
Despite hardship, the combustion maintains
When I felt the hole in my soul
I let go of the reins
In my haze, lost control of the blaze
Despite the time, the wound remains

Letters to Her; Letters to No One
THE QUIET MAN

A man goes forward
Living his life
Endures what burdens him
Glory and strife
He says not a word
Not a single complaint
He's a man of hushed sounds
He's a man with restraint
His hands are gnarled
Knees and elbows worn
Bent, not broken
Damaged, not torn
His eyes see the glory
In all living things
Concrete can't free his soul
It won't give him wings
Overwhelmingly human, he intervenes
The difficulties he's overcome give him Strength
Mortal; his life ends
The quiet man gives in silence
His sacrifices never touted
He does his best to live a life of self-reliance
The quiet man keeps going, even after he's dead
His children still obey him
His wife still doesn't sleep on his side of the bed

Letters to Her; Letters to No One
December 31st

Dear No One,

    I won't turn my back on you. Even when you despise me. I won't give up. I won't give in. Just like you asked me to. How else do you a measure a man, but by his best effort? By his determination?
    It isn't about pride, personal victory or anything of the sort. I simply love you.
    I am more than an aggregation of mistakes.
    So go ahead and move on. I'll watch you as you morph into nothingness. As you pass the threshold. As you disappear beyond the horizon. It changes nothing for me. I will remain.
    I remember a girl who carried a basket full of all her shortcomings and failures. I remember her being so much more than that.
    Can no one see that about me?

Yours truly,
Ian

P.S. It would help if I didn't keep seeing your mom at work.

Letters to Her; Letters to No One
SEPARATED

I'm so close
Lungs ache; burn
Legs pounding, muscles more like wax
I'm not sure how long I'll last
But I can see the prize
Feet fight the incline
Running to walking to stumbling to crawling
Wind blows and beats back
My tears feel like ice
How did everything become so heavy?
When did my clothes become sails?
My fingers lock into the frozen ground
Sweat is dripping off of my nose
Dissenting remarks reverberate
My head is full of them
Arms shakily hold me up
One in front of the other
Go, damn it, go!
I know I can't do this alone
This body is only so capable
I'm spent, prone
"Carry me!"
Please, lift me up
Just a little further
I'm carrying gravity
The majesty of my prize bathes me
"Lift me from this Earth and carry me."
My fingers dig canals
I pull and clench and strain
My defenses, now absent
Exposed to all elements

Carry me

Letters to Her; Letters to No One
CRUSH

My father and I
Watch the contents of the barrel burn
A gleeful ember flies
Free
Soaring
It meets the ground
Vehemently, I stomp the light out

Letters to Her; Letters to No One
WILL

Former soldier
Trained killer
Sinner
All the same
Is he dressed in fatigues with a painted face
Or shackled with irons in a dimly lit place
Or an oven set to make his blood boil
Did he choose this life?
To use his hands for massacre
Did fate choose to give him accuracy
Destiny decide to brashly bestow him
Harmful hands?
When God gave him eagle eyes
Did he even have a choice?

TUNNEL

It's the promises that gave me PTSD
Nothing more demoralizing
Crushing, consuming
Than to run towards the door
And see it
Shrink
It blink into nothing
No sound save for the footfalls
Of brand new heels against
Cold tiled flooring
Nothing so terrifying
As to know your eyes are fine
There is just nothing
To perceive
Spending hours praying for some
Hallucination that can relieve your brain
From being your greatest adversary

Letters to Her; Letters to No One
LIBRARY

They met in the library
She recalls, fingers tracing his spine
At first he belonged to everyone
She selfishly smirks, "You're mine."
Took him home, he never returned
The government charged her
Thirty bucks for a paperback

Letters to Her; Letters to No One
January 1st

Dear No One,

There's a lot going on in my brain. I have a "restless mind." Being pensive was something we both shared. Something I really liked about us.

We could talk about the things that we really loved. What we really wanted out of life. The deepest conversations, though, were always those about what we feared in life.

So now when I sit here, realizing that months have passed, that you're just as happy now as you ever were with me, then I realize I never mentioned the fear that really crippled me.

The murder of those people down the street, so close to my family, made me realize that anything can be taken away from me. So I clenched. I seized up, and suddenly letting you go became this great impossibility.

So when you left, citing me being "bad for you", I lost my mind. The thought that my dedication, that everything I did was so misconstrued... it wrenched me into a fiery anger. I hope you'll understand someday.

I miss you,
Ian

Letters to Her; Letters to No One
Columns PT. II

Melancholy lunar beams
I hear the streams around me
I'm still standing in this field we made
A place of our dreams
As silent is this place
So desolate and not a soul to be found
Even my breaths are resounding
Eyes are wide, waiting
Staving off this thirst, this hunger
It's crushing me, consuming me
The only comfort
Is that there is honor
In patience

CASKET

The desk makes it official
Strong, dark and hand crafted
Beautifully engraved
The man receives it in his office
With a note
"Congratulations on your promotion."
The desk is made of a rare
Desirable
Ebony wood
Everyone is clad in black
The executives
The secretary
She holds a bouquet
The CEO smiles
Hesitant, yet practiced
He says a few words
Everyone is silent
In the end

Letters to Her; Letters to No One
UNIVERSAL

The shock of a paper cut reminds me
Of a particular kind of pain
Punishment for a simple mistake
One small slip
Resolve falters, fails, then fades away
You give up tomorrow to try and save yesterday
Everyone's had that narrow slice in their skin
We all fear it, despite the superficial mark
Just a flesh wound
A through and through
But there is always that sense of foreboding
It won't kill, maim or cripple
It can't
But that sort of pain, on the right day
Makes you wish it had that power

Letters to Her; Letters to No One
CRIME

It is a crime, I take it
I cannot mistake these alleged past acts
I've made pacts, discerned facts from rumors
This moment fills me with rage, a mad dog
In a rabid state, where any movement
Any motion, morose or malicious, provokes
I am trapped despite my innocence
But what is that?
Just because I'm paid to investigate
Means I get the power to close the case?
When they exit, I'm supposed to believe
They get a new life? A blank slate?
But when you're sentenced to life
They take it away, I'm afraid
Afraid of the crime before me
This room dank, dark, disclosing everything
Make it stop spinning
The blood on the walls is coalescing
With images in my mind, and I can see
I can fucking see them dead
All of my loved ones
But I'm paid to keep my cool
Track facts and act professional
Even if it means being an asshole
So who is the real criminal?
The man who plugged these three souls
Who don't realize they're dead?
Or me, the man marking their bodies
Writing neighbor's testimonies
That'll be read in a public court for all
So many will read the papers
But so few their epitaphs
I'm just doing my job
The cost is my humanity

SNOW

Clean and comforting
That glimmering sheen
Fallen on the hardened earth
Nature falls silent
No life
No words as I trudge
Treading through fresh powder
My footfalls are louder
I love this wilting, white world
This pillowy precipitation
Its clean perfection is not snide
Snow touches anything
From the trees to puddles of mud
It lacks all prejudice
Snow reminds me of being a child
Noisy nostalgia amplified around me
I am comforted
I belong here
But in a few days, melts away

Letters to Her; Letters to No One
January 5th

Dear No One,

I've made a list in a little book of every last thing that reminds me of you. It was a bad idea. I keep re-reading it and get choked up every time I do.

But what I love is when people at work or my friends tell me to "just get over" you. If I freaking could, I would. If it were only that simple. If only you were forgettable.

Why couldn't you have just been a pretty face?

Fuck!,
Ian

Letters to Her; Letters to No One
CLOSED AFTER DUSK

I loved it when we spent our nights in cars
Illegally loitering in parks
You laying in my arms
No witnesses but the stars
And the moon above us
Stasis
Nothing more than seatbelts holding us
Back
No tracks on the radio
Just us
Alone
Feature-length make out sessions
To the tune of nocturnal creatures
Naming frogs "Frank" for kicks
Close your eyes and hear it
The heavy breathing
Ducking down at the sound of traffic
Trespassing in parks at night

Letters to Her; Letters to No One
BUTCHER

Full of decadent splendor
Lips parted in a smile
He carves the carcass of morality
Because he doesn't fear
Consequence

Spurning life, his answer is the knife
Cold, clean and calculating
Wetting his lips with a feverish tongue
Not greedily chopping away like a monster
But whittling away deliberately

It was once recognizable
But not anymore
It hardly resembles anything human
Only something that lived
Once

Letters to Her; Letters to No One
MUD

The only constant is
Diminishing
Reduce, retract, redact
While we're growing,
Our boots sink further in the mud

I can't rescue you
When I'm submerged
You're so fucking suffocating
Asphyxiating
But you're all I want to breathe

Go on, let go
Heavy-laden
Over-burdened
I will always let you
Stand on me

Letters to Her; Letters to No One
January 12th

Dear No One,

Every time I think of boots, I think of the place you showed me that summer night. That park where you were fishing, just a little girl.

"I sat here," you said. I immediately plopped down on the pavement just before it. "With my pole and my little steel-toed boots."

I pulled you into my lap to keep you off of the wet asphalt.

Those hints into a life I was waiting to be a part of were floating all around us as we reminisced.

Remembering exactly how the weight of you felt on me and in my arms. How much I wish the sun had been out.

I remember how you smelled, the feeling of the mosquitoes, the subtle swelling of your torso when you inhaled, and the slow deflation when you exhaled. The sound of the water, the residual taste of milk shakes and the muggy, humid air. Everything.

Praying for you,
Ian

Letters to Her; Letters to No One
DANCE

She dances in the wake of flames
A smile on her face
He watches her while
His feet oxidize
Those fiery eyes remind him
How to move
To breathe, to beat brashly against his chest
She topples towering trees
Her hips are swinging while
She is serenely seething
Smoke rises
Monstrous monoliths cover the crimson sky
His ancient eyes observe closely
Roiling pillars, boiling rivers
Seas weep in her presence
As she deftly traverses uneven terrain
Desperately, he does her dance
His joints ache
Pieces of him start
Falling
Fragments flutter to earth
Brittle and useless and spent
He moves to her
Aching to be consumed by those forgiving flames

Letters to Her; Letters to No One
OBSERVING FROM THE EDGE

Trudging along
Trees tremble in the breeze
Step up to the precipice
Wondering, does any man deserve to see so much?
Out there I see the valley
Wild and untamed
No rules nor law to speak
and yet there is prosperity
A straight drop down at my feet
Below, green grass turned gold
In the sky are shapes
Shafts of light shine through the clouds
Columns burdened by the heavens
I am rendered breathless
The air untainted
Is nature as aware of me as I am of it?
Are you?

Letters to Her; Letters to No One
BULL

A lit match gives light
Our young faces bright for the briefest of moments
The wick of the candle ignites
With a wave of her hand, the match goes out
The candle is awakened
Alive
It lights us up as we tell
Stories of the past
Ghost stories
Tall tales
Bullshit
But I can't focus
Because that match
Died to make the candlelight
Its life only served to make another's

Letters to Her; Letters to No One
THE BRINK

Brought back before the brink
With wishes that my frailty will be Exonerated by sincerity

I pause

Frigid, fragile, I look deeply into my reflection
Disconcerted, dismayed, despondent
I am no longer that man
I am no longer the man I was just seconds ago.

Letters to Her; Letters to No One
EMPTY

A rocking chair still feels the momentum
It creeks and groans, bleak and moaning
Its vocalizations gives a history of years of use
The bench swing joins in
On that old wooden porch
The storm is coming
Abandoned
Just the wind blowing as the storm brews
Causes cracks to splinter further
Boards buckle and strain against
Rain
As the winds tear it asunder
Planks and shutters fly
The old cabin takes its leave
With no one to say goodbye

VAULT

Numb hands grasp the handle
Hesitance within him
Bowels squirm and slither around
Eyes closed, he opens the gate
He wonders the tensile strength of his
Nerves
The gate becomes
Unhinged
Because he knows now
The truth uncovered
It's lying there
Just beyond his eyelids

Letters to Her; Letters to No One
DRIVEN

This car has gone far
Traveled hundreds of thousands of miles
It is weathered
Worn by elements of nature
Barely holding together now
How much further does it have?
I ignore that thought
Keep the pedal down and hope for longer
Enough for something to change
To get to where I am going
The engine sputters, fuses glow
Slowing now.
How far to the next exit?
Paint peels, rust and dust decorate the hull
Windshield cracked and splintered
Once burning clean, the exhaust now black
It backfires, then moans
I ignore its cries
I know it hurts, I just need a bit more
Just a bit further and we can rest
Spot the exit, signal right
Another retching, hacking cough
This is the ride's
Final flight

COUP DE GRACE

This is my coup de grace
My homerun swing
My doomsday device
This is my everything
Last rites
Last gasp
A final toast
To late summer nights
Lit by candlelight
Carried by fireflies
I'm all in
My fate will be decided
By a solitary strike

Letters to Her; Letters to No One
January 24th

Dear No One,

All of the mistakes I've made have marked me for a damnation I cannot describe to you. My memory and empathy are a curse.

I can remember everything about you. I can still remember your smell, how you felt, the first time we kissed, and everything. All the special spots in the midst of the night we saw.

Good God, I love you and I can't help it. It might be the only thing I've ever been good at, and even then I failed.

There is a constant fear that I will never have someone that made me feel like you do. I've been on four dates since we split, and nothing meets the standard you've set. No one is good enough.

I give up.

Thinking of you,
Ian

Letters to Her; Letters to No One
THE ILLUSION

Have you ever had a dream
Where your tragedies
Are just stories?
That all the hopes you have had in life
Sit in your lap
That the person you love
Still loves you back
Career is on track
Friends never lied to you
Or died on you
Eyes bolt open in panic
With a thumping heart
Drenched in sweat
All thirsts quenched
But it's fleeting
The fallacy that everything is all right
Evaporates
Futilely clinging with a vice grip
False reality starts to slip
You hurriedly get up
Run to the phone
Dial their numbers only to realize
You're alone

Letters to Her; Letters to No One
THE LEDGER

The father's hand grasps
Whiskey on the shelf
Picked up as a gift for the newlyweds
This dreaded day has come
His baby's all grown up
She should fill her cup and be merry
Eyes pass over picture
Freckled blond girl in an orange dress
He pays

The bottle sits in the cupboard
From neglect, dust sets, collects
One day, there's laughter
Light shines through as the door splays ajar
Young, slender hand retrieves, uncaps, pours
Amber liquid in two glasses
Fire water prior to amours

Returned now, dust settles again
Used to it
Aged twelve years, what's another few?
There's another echoing laugh, is it time
Again grasped by the neck and pulled
Into the light
Now it's brought to the shore
A bonfire with couples laughing
Shambling back to the cabin
Drunkenly staggering up stone steps

It's been two years since that night
Alone in its two cubic foot home
It's waiting for the perfect occasion
Half full, optimistic, an aged bottle
But something says, "ingest my sultry soul"
Something's different this time

Young woman and tears
Young man departs
The bottle's been here all the while
Ol' reliable, faithful, never lets her down
So fast; she's famished
The burning soothes, or so it hopes

Her eyes pass over the pictures
The wedding
The honeymoon
Immortalizations of when they couldn't fail
Wearily weeping and missing those days
She pays

Letters to Her; Letters to No One
February 14th

Dear No One,

    I dreamt we were fine. I woke up thinking, for just the longest second on earth, that we were just okay and I checked my phone with the dumbest expectation that you'd messaged me with something sweet for me to wake up to.
    Shit...
    The best part? We were finally going to the science center... with your whole family. I was going to brag about how my grandfather worked on the Mercury space probe.
    This sucks.

Trying to let go,
Ian

Letters to Her; Letters to No One
GRIP

Rusty, golden, brown and burnt orange
Shakily trying their best
A test of endurance
But eventually, they relent
Hesitantly, the first is a spent yellow one
It swings down wearily
Another follows after, and another
Until, like fictionalized lemmings
Leaves blanket the ground
Until the old, tall thing sleeps
Bared in the cold for months
But someday, it will awake
It will be vibrant again
All it can do right now is survive
Even though it has lost all of its friends
It will live

Letters to Her; Letters to No One
March 15th

Dear No One,

 I ran over a cat today on my way home from work on 66. I never take 66, but today I decided to, the road time I figured would help me think and clear my head - which has become more and more of a necessity these days.
 I didn't see it coming - not even close. I pulled off to the side of the road and thankfully, it was already dead. I went to Wally world and picked up a shovel, came back and buried it on the side of the road, got back in my car and cried for a solid thirty minutes.
 The image of that animal, lying there, wouldn't leave my mind.
 It had no idea it was going to die today. No clue its life would end. What's the difference between me and that cat? I like to think I have a better mind for assessing danger, and that I am more survivable. But all it takes is one thing.
 A car going too fast, some punk with a gun. For all I know, I've got a tumor growing in the confines of my brain.
 So then I wonder what the hell I'm doing. What the fuck is the point of raising my expectations? I have "plans" in my head. Dreams, hopes, things I hope to accomplish.
 But there's a good chance I'll never realize that - if only because I rely on someone else to fulfill them. I didn't think you would leave - I thought I had everything set. But then it happened, didn't it?
 When did I become such a pussy? Did you soften me so much?
 So after my cry, I finally got home and held my cat. I managed to not weep, but I just pet her and realized: I am just a man. I am capable, like all others, of sin and ugliness.

It doesn't make me regret much, now. The fear of the future and losing it is infantile and irrational. All it does is make me regret.

If I had known this was how it would end, and I had a chance to go back knowing that I couldn't change the outcome other than stopping it from happening altogether, would I?

I can honestly say I wouldn't. I would love you more. More than I already did. I would have held you closer, longer, more lovingly. I would have written longer letters, told you how much I loved you twice as often, I would have made you feel beautiful not just every day, but every hour. As often as I could. I would take every single last chance of seeing you, and let my eyes drink you in, knowing there was a finite amount I was going to get.

So I guess, in the long run, you win. Haha, isn't that the greatest?

-Ian

Made in the USA
Lexington, KY
06 June 2016